BELIEVER'S BAPTISM

"This book is a treasure chest of biblical information, spiritual insight and practical suggestions. Pastor Joel has made a subject that too much of the time we have made complicated into something that makes sense and is easily understood. He deals very honestly and biblically with some of the real issues that have so unnecessarily divided believers by providing a firm scriptural foundation while recognizing the diversity that truly exists in the body of Christ. You will not be disappointed by using this tool to help ground believers and enable their growth in discipleship."

Dr. John P. Holsey
Speaker, Teacher and Trainer

"I already experienced how this book is helpful to prepare someone for his or her baptism. I liked the added historical review. I also liked (but was not surprised at all) how you wrote from a perspective respectful towards diverse experience and diverse traditions. The 'personal testimony' section is also extremely helpful."

Ryung S. Kim, MDiv. PhD.
Associate Professor and Pastor
Albert Einstein College of Medicine

"I recently had the privilege to do some baptisms with Pastor Joel here in Thailand. He has a heart to see people be baptized, but also for people to understand the true meaning behind it. This book will help you understand the root meaning and history of baptism in water. This is a great resource for churches and missionaries. It's written in a way that's clear and easily understood. We are excited to be using it as a resource among the Isaan people in Thailand."

Lazaro Ical Barrera
Missionary Pastor
Hopewell Asia Missions

"I appreciated how you emphasized how baptism is 'an outward demonstration of an inward transformation.' This is such an important distinction to make because of historical confusion about the meaning of baptism. I am glad that 'the transformational nature of baptism' is the story that you convey in your book. What I appreciated the most about the book, for purely practical purposes, was the part about the reasons that we are baptized. Of course, I was familiar with some of the material because I had used an early version of it last fall when I met with four young people who we baptized in September. I found it helpful to review these reasons with the students last fall and I appreciated how each of them included their reason(s) in their faith story which was read before they were baptized."

Jim Laverty, MDiv.
Lead Pastor
Mountville Mennonite Church

"*My mentor and friend C. Peter Wagner was fond of saying, 'Whatever we assume people know will be ignored.' The basics of Christianity cannot be ignored. If there was ever an important time for practical, contemporary expression of Biblical truth on the historical tenets of Christianity it is now when many of the millennial age group have been influenced by other than Biblical sources. Joel Kolb is a solid Bible teacher and he brings his skills to help us understand water baptism. I love that Joel teaches in such a practical manner because many seeking baptism will be new converts without Bible knowledge.*"

Brian Sauder, M.A.
Director of Dove/ Hopewell Leadership Training School
Apostolic Council of DOVE International

"*The author, Pastor Joel Kolb, has written on this important subject in such a way that any new believer, or believer that wants to rededicate their life, can understand. He explains with such clarity both the historical understanding of believer's baptism in the church and the personal application for any person today. He answers questions and prompts thoughts to allow a believer to experience their baptism in a very meaningful way. I highly recommend this book for every believer in Jesus Christ!*"

Curt Malizzi
Senior Pastor
Hopewell Christian Fellowship

"Believer's Baptism is an excellent survey of baptism in general and believer's baptism in particular. It is a practical format that can be easily adapted for a variety of settings. The workbook section is a good interactive resource. Believer's Baptism is an easy-to-use resource for those who are interested in baptism."

Allan Yoder
Senior Pastor
Good Shepherd Community Church

"Pastor Joel's book on baptism is a great resource for churches. In clear and personal language, he provides an overview of how baptism has been practiced in the church, offers a workbook that prepares candidates for baptism, responds to common questions about the ritual, and even includes a guide to baptismal services. I have no doubt that pastors and church leaders alike will find this book very helpful."

Derek Cooper, PhD
Associate Professor of World Christian History
Biblical Theological Seminary

"*Joel Kolb's new book, Believer's Baptism, is a great read for those in the process of being baptized in water. It is also a great resource for those who are actually administering the water baptism service. This book is skillfully written and is interactive with the reader, properly preparing a new believer for water baptism. The explanation of the difference between water baptism and Holy Spirit baptism is clear and biblically sound. Thank you, Joel, for this practical tool that you have written to help the whole body of Christ, regardless of denomination or church affiliation.*"

Larry Kreider
DOVE International Director and Author

Endless Press
15 S Church St
Spring City, PA 19475
Info@EndlessPress.org
www.EndlessPress.org

ISBN 978-1545234686

This book is typeset in Alegreya and Cambria fonts.

I would like to dedicate this book to the memory of my maternal grandfather, Elton B. Meyers. I received from him his name, his love for the Bible and a model of a transformed life.

BELIEVER'S BAPTISM

by J. Elton Kolb

Endless
Press
EndlessPress.org

Contents

Preface

When I was a new pastor I was asked to participate in giving instruction to our baptismal candidates. The senior pastor handed me a list of scripture verses to use for the class. As I searched the scriptures I found that there was much more to the subject than I previously thought. I wanted to simply explain baptism to those who desired to be baptized, but the more I read and researched, the more questions I had.

Over more than a decade and a half of pastoral ministry and missions experience, I have had the privilege of baptizing many people both old and young. I have been allowed to participate in baptism of believers in countries like India and Thailand where this declaration of faith comes at a higher cost. I have witnessed the richness of this experience and the power for personal transformation. This is more than a routinely conducted religious ritual. It is a powerful transformative encounter.

There are many scholarly works on the subject of baptism, but not many practical resources. This book was originally written as a baptismal instruction workbook. A few years ago I also wrote an essay for a church history class in graduate school which I wanted to incorporate into the book. After sharing my work with a few colleagues, I was encouraged to revise and publish the booklet for a wider audience.

How To Use This Book

It is my hope that this book will be a resource for pastors and baptismal candidates to use in preparation for baptism. The first part of the book is an essay describing the history of baptism from biblical times to modern day. This provides a context for understanding believer's baptism as it relates to other baptismal traditions. The second part is a workbook which is designed to be read and completed by the baptismal candidate.

I typically conduct baptism instruction in two sessions. In the first session, we talk about the various imagery and reasons for baptism, and I then assign the testimony writing exercise as homework. In the second session, I have the students practice sharing their testimony with the group. Then I answer specific questions they may have and talk about what will happen during the ceremony. For younger children or adults with learning disabilities, I prefer letting the parents or teachers use the book to give instruction, after which I conduct a simple interview to hear their testimony and to answer questions.

My Baptism Story

In this book I encourage the baptismal candidate to write and share their personal testimony. As we look at the subject of baptism it might be helpful for you to know about my own journey of faith in Christ and baptism.

Like some people who have been baptized as children, I was one of those people who have been a Christian as long as I can remember. I came to faith in Christ as a child, although I don't remember exactly when that happened. My parents tell me I was invited along with my older siblings to a neighbor's Child Evangelism crusade. I came home and reported that I asked Jesus into my heart.

At that time, we were part of the Mennonite church which taught that children could not make a genuine commitment to Christ until they reached a certain age where they could fully understand the gospel. My parents wondered if it could be true that I had really been converted at such a young age. I was only about five years old. Nevertheless, they noticed a change in my attitude and behavior from that day forward. While I do not remember that particular event, I do remember beginning a personal relationship with Jesus from a very young age.

I was the youngest of seven children, and as the youngest I often felt powerless to know how to handle the teasing of my older siblings. I would often 'run away.' By that I mean I would disappear into the woods of our family farm until dinnertime or until it became dark outside. During those times I would walk and talk with God.

I had heard in Sunday School that you could talk to God like you would to any other person. So I did. I told God all about my feelings and frustrations, and God would talk to me in a not necessarily audible, but understandable way. I held conversations out loud, interspersed with songs and reciting scripture from memory. It was there that God first gave me a vision for my life and called me to the ministry. My childlike faith was forming a spiritual transformation in me.

I also remember asking about baptism at an early age. I would guess that I was around the age of seven. I remember at least one conversation about it on the way to school. I was told that I was too young to really know what it means to be a Christian. They called it "the age of accountability." It was supposed to coincide with the Jewish practice of Bar Mitzvah. As a child I was considered to be innocent, not yet aware of sin. However, I had at that age both the awareness of sin and the desire to demonstrate repentance. The church, on the other hand, did not have a theological category for my experience. At that time there was such a resistance to the idea of baptizing children that there was no means for affirming the believing heart of the child.

I was baptized routinely at the age of twelve along with at least one of my closest peers, yet it was a meaningful experience. Our church practiced baptism by pouring. As the water ran down my back it sent a chill up my spine. I knew that the physical act was symbolic of a supernatural cleansing. I wondered if my friend who was baptized at the same time felt the same way I did. He didn't talk about God much. In fact he behaved very differently at home than he did at church. But then, neither of us was perfect. In the years ahead we both had our times of backsliding, his lasted much longer than mine. Both of us are walking with the Lord today.

During those years of childhood, I often wrestled with knowing if I was really saved. Some people would say that once you were saved, you were always saved. Others would say that you could never really be sure and it was best to ask God to forgive you often and for everything just to be safe. Each summer I would go to church camp and rededicate my life to the Lord. The good feeling would last for a few months and then the guilt and doubt would begin all over again.

The summer after my baptism I had a different experience. My parents were involved in the early Charismatic movement and I would often tag along to meetings where people would have powerful experiences which they called "the baptism of the Holy Spirit." I didn't know what to think of all that, but I wanted to know God better. I wanted to know Him like I did walking in the woods as a child. I told my counselor that year that I wanted to be transformed like Peter who went from being the cowardly disciple who denied Jesus to the powerful preacher at Pentecost. God filled me with the Holy Spirit that very night.

It was that same feeling of being closer to God that I had experienced each summer, but beyond anything I had ever felt before. From that moment on I knew I was saved. I don't know how I knew, except for the joy that I felt inside. I just knew.

I told my mother about my experience on the way home from camp. She smiled knowingly and said, "What you experienced is the baptism of the Holy Spirit." She added, "Now if you find that you are suddenly praying in a language that you don't know or have never learned, that is the gift of tongues. Just know that it is a gift from the Holy Spirit to help you as you pray."

Three weeks later it happened as I was raking hay on a warm summer evening. I often sang on the tractor as I was sure no one could hear me over the noise of the motor. Still feeling the joy of my camp experience I found myself singing some strange words. I thought perhaps my mother's suggestion had influenced me, so I tried to stop. Moments later it began again and I decided to just go along with it. The next day my father asked what had happened to me the night before. I wondered how he could possibly know since I had not told anyone. He told me that he had just tried to bale the field of hay where I was working and the rows were so crooked that they were hard to follow! He was delighted to hear the reason.

I found that through high school there were very few who understood or could relate to my story. My wife was the exception. At the time she was just a friend who sought me out because she too had experienced the baptism of the Holy Spirit. On one of her first notes to me she described the Holy Sprit's presence as being like "a warm blanket on a cold night." Through the years I have encountered many who have experienced the Holy Spirit, but who have not had a vocabulary with which to describe their own encounter. Some spoke in tongues and some did not, but each one comes away with the certainty that they have encountered God in a way which meant they will never be the same again.

I decided to attend a Pentecostal Bible school after high school. I wanted to know more about the Holy Spirit and learn from people who seemed to know more than those in my faith tradition. However, while in school I attended a local Baptist church because it felt more like what I was used to. I wanted to become a member of the church, but that would have required being re-baptized. Baptism by immersion was a core doctrine of this church. Since I had been baptized in the Mennonite church by pouring, they would not transfer my membership without re-administering the rite.

I believe strongly in being a member of a local church, so I decided to inquire of my Mennonite pastor back home. He supported my desire to be part of that church but advised that if I were to be baptized it should not be for the sake of methodology, but true conviction. Baptism and church membership in this case, were being used in a way that was not bringing the Body of Christ together, but forcing me to choose whose side I would be on. I have fellowshipped with a number of different churches and denominations through the years and each has added to my understanding of the gospel and of Christ.

To this day I have not been re-baptized by immersion. I would not object to doing so if I felt that God was leading me to do it, but I would need a reason other than methodology. I continue to walk in the new life in Christ that was attested at my baptism. Yes, there have been some ups and downs along the way. God has always been faithful in bringing me back to the relationship I had with Him from a very young age.

These experiences have both prompted and guided my research on the subject of baptism. I believe that baptism is more than just a ritual. It is an outward demonstration of an inner transformation. Most discussions of baptism are designed to defend a particular tradition. My story both challenges and affirms aspects of the tradition in which I was raised. My hope is to promote the biblical concept of believer's baptism while shedding some of the traditional baggage that has accumulated along the way. I know that personal experiences will differ, but the transformational nature of baptism is the story that I want to convey.

A Brief History of Baptism

The ceremony in which you are about to participate has a very long and rich tradition. People have risked their lives to be baptized while others have been forced to receive baptism under penalty of death. It has long been disputed how one should be baptized, when one should be baptized, and what affect this event has on the one being baptized. Is it just a symbolic event or is there a real power for transformation released in this experience? Those questions have been the subject of many books. It is my goal, in these few short pages, to help you appreciate the richness of this tradition and to expand the multi-faceted nature of your baptism experience. I pray that you experience the fullness of Christ at your baptism!

Baptism In Biblical Times

The practice of baptism predates Christianity. The first mention of baptism in the Bible is the ministry of John the Baptist. The scripture says: *"Then Jerusalem and all Judea and all the region about the Jordan were going out to him, and they were baptized by him in the river Jordan, confessing their sins."* (Matthew 3:5-6). Now we know that somewhere along the way, Jews began using baptism as a means of marking the conversion of proselytes to Judaism. Whether this was the case before John the Baptist is difficult to say[1]. The Old Testament purification laws required a person to bathe after a period of illness or contact with something unclean. Baptism, from its earliest practice would have been understood as a cleansing of the conscience from sin just like washing dirt from the body.

John the Baptist's ministry was essentially a spiritual revival for the Jews of his day. They were already part of Israel, the people of God, but because they were under Roman rule and surrounded by heathen culture, they constantly struggled to maintain their spiritual heritage and identity. It was no coincidence that John chose the Jordan River for his baptism services[2]. This was the place where God parted the waters for the second time and the children of Israel entered their promised land. For those who desired to respond to John's call to repentance, this signaled a new beginning. They were entering, once again and wholeheartedly, the plan and purpose of God.

Now it might seem odd that Jesus also came to be baptized. He did not need to be cleansed from sin. In fact, John was reluctant to baptize him.[3]. By doing so, Jesus was identifying with us in his humanity, but it also seems clear that Jesus wanted to be identified with this new movement. After being baptized, Jesus travelled the land proclaiming that a new kingdom, the "Kingdom of God," was inaugurated. This event, as the story is now told, marked the beginning of Jesus's public ministry.

After Jesus was raised from the dead, he commissioned his followers by telling them: *"Go therefore and make disciples of all the nations, baptizing them in the name of the Father and of the Son and of the Holy Spirit."* (Matthew 28:19). Baptism became the means by which people are identified as followers of Jesus. We see in the book of Acts that as people come to faith in Christ they are baptized to mark their conversion. This included Gentiles, such as the household of Cornelius (Acts 10:47-48), as well as Jews like Saul (Paul) of Tarsus (Acts 9:18).

Baptism In The Early Church

The Bible does not tell us all we may want to know about baptism. It does not describe the method of baptism in any detail and it does not give the exact words that were spoken or the content of the instruction that was received. The earliest source for this information comes from a historical document which was discovered in 1873. The *Didache* is widely believed to be a collection of sayings from the 12 Apostles which was hand copied by a monk around the turn of the first millennium and then lost for over 800 years[4]. It contains the following instruction regarding baptism:

> *"Concerning baptism, you should baptize this way: After first explaining all things, baptize in the name of the Father, and of the Son, and of the Holy Spirit, in flowing water. But if you have no running water; and if you cannot do so in cold water, then in warm. If you have very little, pour water three times on the head in the name of the Father and Son and Holy Spirit. Before the baptism, both the baptizer and the candidate for baptism, plus any others who can should fast. The candidate should fast one or two days before hand[5]."*

The Didache shows us that there was room for diversity in the first century church as to the means of baptism. The Apostles were being practical by suggesting that the water should be flowing and/or cold. Stagnant or warm water would be the more likely to carry disease. It indicated that not all baptisms were by immersion, though it may still seem to be preferred. Baptism was not entered into lightly or without prior teaching as to its significance. The instructions regarding fasting were to mark this as a solemn occasion by both the recipient and the larger community.

In the centuries that followed the first Apostles, Christianity was not officially recognized as a legal religion. There were no church buildings or denominational headquarters. There were only those who heard the story of Jesus and who had received the Holy Spirit from someone who had received it from someone who was with Jesus. The Bible, as we know it, would be later compiled from the various tracts and letters that were circulating in those days. Christians were united by a few simple creeds and especially by the declaration that "Jesus is Lord!" Those who belonged to this group were often persecuted or even killed for their faith in Jesus Christ. As one author sums it up, "Christianity was largely a personal experience spontaneously shared by individuals[6]." Baptism continued to be the primary way the people were voluntarily identified as believers in Christ and members of this community.

As Christianity was entering into the second and third century, and as children were being born to Christian parents, the practice of baptizing children also emerged. It is unclear at what age they were baptized or for what reason. Scholars have often failed to distinguish between a baptism of an infant that is/was initiated by the parents and what may have been a voluntary act on the part of a child, even very young children[7]. Most of the references from the second century which refer to child baptism are usually taken as referencing infant baptism, but that is not necessarily the case[8]. The early church Fathers frequently exhort that some kind of instruction should precede baptism, which suggests that baptism was normally reserved for believers.

The practice of baptizing infants as a rite of initiation into the church, as is the custom in the Catholic, Lutheran and some Reformed churches, seems to have originated in North Africa around the beginning of the third century. It is first mentioned by Origen (184/185 – 253/254) and later popularized by Augustine (354-430)[9]. This form of infant baptism (sometimes referred to as "paedobaptism") emphasizes the covenant relationship between God and His people. Just as Jewish custom called for circumcision of infant sons, baptism became the equivalent symbol of the Christian covenant[10].

Because baptism was believed to be an act of spiritual regeneration and cleansing of the sinful nature, it was generally administered only once in a lifetime. Tertullian opposed the practice of baptizing children, recommending that they wait until puberty when they can best learn what it means to be a Christian[11]. By this time also, baptism had taken on some "mystical" or overly superstitious meaning. There are some examples of people who waited until later in life to be baptized, believing that if they fell into sin after being baptized it may negate their conversion.

As Christianity became recognized as a legitimate religion, and quickly became the official religion of Rome, baptism became intertwined with political objectives. Whereas the first three centuries saw people risking their lives to be baptized, the fourth century brought baptisms which were socially convenient and sometimes forced on people. In the 9th century Charlemagne, the first king to be appointed by the Pope, took it even further by demanding that conquered people groups be baptized or be killed, and that they should baptize their infants, making them "Christians"[12]. For some time, it would be difficult to know or to discern whether this was an individual, voluntary expression of faith in Christ or simply wanting to be identified with the social or political majority.

Baptism and the Reformation

While the early church received the grace and power of God through a network of relationships and the continuity of apostolic leaders, years of fallen leaders and corrupt motives produced a system of rituals which were supposed to make people into Christians[13]. The Protestant Reformation brought a resurgence of emphasis on personal saving faith. Reformers like Martin Luther and Ulrich Zwingli taught that salvation is by faith alone and is affirmed by, but not achieved through, the ordinances of the church[14]. However, the child mortality rate was very high in those days and people wanted to know that their children would go to heaven if they died at an early age. Infant baptism continued in most of the early Protestant traditions utilizing the covenant theology of the Catholic Church.

Another group of reformers which emerged from the first group questioned the practice of infant baptism. By this time, the Bible was available in print and could be read in multiple languages. The "Anabaptists," as they were called, read in the scripture that people were baptized after believing in Christ. In a house meeting in Zurich, Switzerland in 1527, Conrad Grebel, a student of Zwingli, baptized another member of the group, who in turn baptized the rest of the group[15]. This brought immediate persecution by the state-sponsored church because it threatened to undo the social structure that was built around church membership which was inherently part of the meaning of baptism at the time.

Instead of quenching the new movement, it began to spread westward over Europe. Baptism was once again a voluntary act of submission to Christ that could come at a great cost as it did in the early church. Later that year the surviving Anabaptist leaders identified seven principles on which they disagreed with the current reformation, the first of which was baptism. This is from the Schlietheim Confession of 1527:

> *"Baptism shall be given to all those who have been taught repentance ...and who believe truly that their sins are taken away through Christ, and to all those who desire to walk in the resurrection of Jesus Christ and be buried with Him in death, so that they might rise with Him; to all those who understanding themselves desire and request it from us; hereby excluded all infant baptism[16]."*

Believer's Baptism In Modern Times

Today, many people have never heard of Anabaptists (which simply means "baptized again"). We now know them as Mennonites, Amish and Brethren, just to name a few of the denominations which emerged from this group. Perhaps the largest proponents of believer's baptism today are called Baptists. These are indirectly derived from Anabaptism. Their founder, John Smyth, baptized himself after he learned the practice from Mennonites in Amsterdam while fleeing persecution from the Church of England[17]. As people became more individualistic and free-thinking, the traditional view of baptism as an initiation rite gave way to a newer, or rather an older, view of baptism[18] as an outer expression of an inner transformation[19]. Both Baptists and Anabaptists brought their understanding of conversion and baptism to the New World. Believer's baptism is now widely practiced across many church denominations. Child dedication has replaced infant baptism in many of these traditions.

The church where I serve, Hopewell Christian Fellowship, comes from the Anabaptist and Mennonite traditions. The 1963 Mennonite Confession of Faith states:

> *"We regard water baptism as an ordinance of Christ which symbolizes the baptism of the Holy Spirit, divine cleansing from sin and its guilt, identification with Christ in His death and resurrection and commitment to follow Him in a life of faithful discipleship[20]."*

During the Charismatic movement of the 1980's, Hopewell Mennonite Church in Elverson, PA experienced an outpouring of the Holy Spirit which resulted in a series of church-plants. This was the beginning of the Hopewell Network of Churches. The Hopewell churches experience baptism as a time of celebration, where many people who may have thought this was just an old, traditional ceremony are baptized in the context of a living faith community and encounter the presence of God.

What is your church's history? Do you know the story of how your church or denomination came to be? Every tradition was born out of a time of revival in the church. There are reasons for the way that we worship and conduct our services which are tied to our history and often have rich meaning. This is a good time to learn about your faith community and it's unique story.

Believer's Baptism Workbook

Baptism is a special time in your life when you affirm your commitment to Jesus Christ. There can be a number of reasons for wanting to be baptized and there are multiple meanings or ways that a person might think about baptism. You might also be wondering what will happen at your baptism and what you will be expected to know or do.

This workbook is designed to help you prepare for baptism. You will learn what the Bible says about baptism and what it means. You will find out what will happen at your baptism and you will be asked questions that will help you to discover and understand what this experience means to you.

What Does It Mean To Be Baptized?

Baptism is an outward expression of an inward transformation.

The Meaning of the Word 'Baptism'

The word baptism comes from the Greek word baptizō (*bap-tid'-zo*) which literally means to be dipped or immersed. Water baptism involves getting wet, and more than just a little wet. Whenever possible, a person who is baptized will become completely saturated as they are submerged in water.

The idea of being completely "into" something is at the heart of what it means to be baptized. You can be immersed in a book, in a project, or in an experience. When you are in that state, it is the only thing that matters.

When you are baptized as a believer in water, you are baptized into Christ. He is all that matters. Your baptism demonstrates that you have made Jesus both Savior and Lord of your life. The purpose of your baptism is to reinforce, both publicly and personally, your commitment to Christ.

When have you most recently committed or re-dedicated your life to Christ?

_____

_____

_____

The Imagery of Baptism

Baptism is a demonstration of what happens when a person believes in Jesus. It is an "acting out" of what is taking place spiritually. These images help the person being baptized, and those who witness the event, realize what has happened and what is happening in the life of the one being baptized.

Baptism is a multi-faceted experience; it will mean different things to different people at different times. Like a cut diamond, each time you look at it you can see something new. The Bible uses a number of images to describe what happens in baptism. One or more of these may be especially meaningful to you now. You will come to see and appreciate the others more as you grow in your walk with Christ.

The image of cleansing - The most obvious image of baptism in the Bible is that of cleansing, bathing, or rinsing away one's sins. In Bible times, washing was sometimes a religious activity. The laver, a large washbasin, was part of the Old Testament tabernacle furniture. Ceremonial washing was practiced by many Pharisees at the time of Jesus. In Judaism there is also a form of immersion (Mikvah) which is used for ceremonial cleansing. John baptized people as a symbolic act of turning from sin and toward God, yet this was a mere foreshadowing of the cleansing which would come through Christ.

"I baptize you with water for repentance, but he who is coming after me is mightier than I, whose sandals I am not worthy to carry. He will baptize you with the Holy Spirit and fire. (Matthew 3:11)

The image of re-birth - When Jesus spoke with Nicodemus he used the metaphor of natural birth as an analogy of spiritual transformation. When a baby comes into the world it is surrounded by water until birth. Because both natural birth and baptism involve emerging from water, it becomes an illustration of spiritual rebirth. The infant emerges from the water and takes its first breath. This is also a picture of what it means to be born again. The water stands for repentance and the first breath for the spiritual life that God gives to us.

Jesus answered, "Truly, truly, I say to you, unless one is born of water and the Spirit, he cannot enter the kingdom of God. That which is born of the flesh is flesh, and that which is born of the Spirit is spirit. Do not marvel that I said to you, 'You must be born again.'" (John 3:5-7)

Rites of initiation - Baptism is generally known as a rite of initiation into a religious group. This is supported in scripture and by church tradition. From the earliest days of Christianity, baptism was used as ceremonial entry into the church. Some older traditions even locate their baptistery at the entrance of the church to symbolize baptism as the point of entry into the faith.

In the Bible, baptism associated a person with the one in whose name, or under whose authority, they were said to be baptized. Some believers are described as being baptized into the name of either John or Paul or Jesus. In fact, Paul had to clarify to the Corinthian believers that his purpose in baptizing was not to create a following after himself (1 Cor. 1:14-17).

We baptize believers into the body of Jesus Christ. In some denominations, that means becoming a member of the local church. More importantly, it means that they belong to the group of people worldwide who have trusted Jesus Christ for their salvation.

> *On hearing this, they were baptized in the name of the Lord Jesus.* (Acts 19:5)

Rites of passage - As we look back on our lives certain events stand out as being the milestone or turning point by which we can identify change. Going to school, getting your driver's license, or getting married are all events which mark a permanent change in your life, propelling you toward your destiny. Baptism is also a rite of passage.

When the children of Israel passed through the Red Sea it would have been viewed as the point of no return on their journey. Baptism should be one of those moments in your life when you experience change. This does not mean that everything changes instantly, nor does it mean that you will never experience old temptaions or habits. What it does, however, is make a public declaration of your intent to follow Jesus. There is power in the declaration of your will; the community lends its support to your testimony and God responds with empowering grace. Looking back from a distance, we hope you will see that baptism marks a significant milestone in your spiritual journey.

> *For I do not want you to be unaware, brothers that our fathers were all under the cloud, and all passed through the sea, and all were baptized into Moses in the cloud and in the sea. (1 Corinthians 10:1-2)*

The imagery of covering - The literal meaning of baptism is to immerse. Whenever you dip or immerse something, it becomes covered with that in which it was dipped or immersed. The implication is that by doing so a change takes place.

When forging steel, the steel is placed in fire until it glows red. This makes the steel soft enough to shape with a hammer. Then it is cooled quickly in water, changing the molecular structure of the steel and making its new form permanent and very hard to break.

Baptism in water is a picture of your Spiritual formation and transformation. It is symbolic of baptism in Christ and the person who is baptized becomes covered with Christ. You put on Christ as you would a garment so that when God looks at you, He sees Christ.

For as many of you as were baptized into Christ have put on Christ. (Galatians 3:27)

The imagery of dying and rising again - Our understanding of salvation through faith in Jesus Christ relies upon the image of the substitutionary sacrifice that was made by Jesus for our sin. Just as the Old Testament sacrifices in the temple provided atonement for sin, Jesus is our atoning sacrifice made once and for all. As believers we relate to Christ's death and resurrection as it becomes a metaphor that describes our conversion experience (Gal. 2:20).

The baptism process "acts out" this scenario of dying, being buried beneath the water, and rising up out of the water as a means of graphically identifying with what Christ has done. The thought of bringing someone to the point of death only to revive them again in order to demonstrate their salvation may sound ridiculous, but that is essentially what baptism portrays. Just as someone who has had a near death experience lives differently because of what is realized at that moment, so should the person who is baptized come away with a new appreciation for the true meaning and purpose of their life.

We were buried therefore with him by baptism into death, in order that, just as Christ was raised from the dead by the glory of the Father, we too might walk in newness of life. (Romans 6:4)

The imagery of being saved - Being saved implies escaping destruction. There are verses in the Bible which compare water baptism to the experience of Noah and his family during the flood. They were preserved while water destroyed the corruption that was on the earth. They were the first ones to literally be "saved." This term is commonly used by evangelicals to describe our conversion to Christianity.

Use of the term "saved" recognizes that without Christ we would all be destroyed by our sin. Thank God that, in Christ, we have a new life and a living hope! The passage below is not saying that baptism literally saves us, because we know that we are saved by faith in Jesus Christ; the imagery of baptism is that we are rescued while our sin nature is destroyed.

> ... when God's patience waited in the days of Noah, while the ark was being prepared, in which a few, that is, eight persons, were brought safely through water. Baptism, which corresponds to this, now saves you, not as a removal of dirt from the body but as an appeal to God for a good conscience, through the resurrection of Jesus Christ, (1 Peter 3:20-21)

Baptism is a multi-faceted experience. As you review the biblical imagery, some of these will stand out to you because of your own unique perspective. How you understand baptism will be affected by what is happening in your life right now. Later, you may look back on your baptism and appreciate it again from a different point of view.

Which of these images is most meaningful to you right now and why?

_____

_____

_____

_____

_____

_____

_____

_____

_____

_____

_____

_____

_____

Why do you want to be baptized?

Baptism is an outward expression of an inward transformation, which means that believing is a requirement for baptism. Throughout the history of the church many people were baptized without either understanding its meaning or giving consent. The Bible, however, presents baptism as an experience that is an expression of personal faith in God, which is why we practice believer's baptism.

Your reasons for being baptized are vitally important. According to Mark 16:16, believing plus baptism equals salvation. The two experiences, the inner transformation and the outward demonstration, should work together to produce a completely changed individual. To baptize an infant or an adult who has not made a commitment to Christ does not attest to a personal salvation experience. If you are to be baptized as a believer it is important to know what has brought you to this decision.

Valid reasons for being baptized

The following are some reasons for being baptized which can be supported from scripture. Each one reflects an aspect of personal transformation. Which of the following statements expresses your desire for baptism?

- I am making a declaration of my intent to follow Christ (Acts 22:16).
- I want to be baptized as an act of obedience to Christ by doing what is right (Matt 3:15).
- I want to mark a turning point in my life (John 3:5).
- I want to be baptized as part of a process of spiritual restoration (Acts 9:17-19).
- I want to experience a greater freedom and deliverance from things associated with my past (Acts 2:38).
- I want to enhance my spiritual life by identifying with Christ's death and resurrection (Rom 6:4).
- I want to be assured of my salvation (Mark 16:16).
- I have recommitted my life to Christ (Acts 2:41).
- I want to be baptized as a believer having a fuller revelation of what baptism means (Acts 19:5)
- I want to demonstrate my spiritual transformation by identifying with Christ's death and resurrection (Rom6:4).
- I have another reason:

_____

_____

_____

_____

Your confession of faith

Normally and historically, believer's baptism is administered after hearing a candidate's confession of faith. This is most often done by sharing a testimony publicly or at least in the presence of those administering the baptism. A confession of faith is your declaration of intent to follow Christ. It is a testimony to the truth of the gospel and the resulting change in your life.

How are we to know that you have made a commitment of your life to Jesus Christ? What evidence is there that the inward part of your transformation has taken place? Here are a few things that a person administering baptism would want to know or observe:

Your confession of faith - Have you asked Jesus to forgive your sin and to be your Savior and Lord? How and when did this happen? (Acts 16:31)

Your personal transformation - What was your life like before and after you accepted Jesus? Were there changes that happened immediately that made you aware of a difference in your life? Was there a change in your attitude and perspective on life? Did other people notice a change? (2 Cor 5:17)

The witness of the Spirit - Someone who was raised in a stable Christian environment might not think they had a dramatic salvation experience. Their life was already influenced by the gospel before they believed, so there is instead an inner witness of the Spirit for what has taken place. The Holy Spirit, who was primarily an agent of conviction before salvation, becomes your friend and companion. You simply know that you are saved. (Gal 4:6)

Your life bears the fruit of salvation - Just as a plant bears fruit after its kind, when our lives are joined to Christ we live godly lives (John 15:4). Our attitudes and actions reflect the fruit of the Spirit listed in Gal 5:22-23.

On the next page you will have an opportunity to write out your testimony. First Peter 3:15 says, *"but in your hearts honor Christ the Lord as holy, always being prepared to make a defense to anyone who asks you for a reason for the hope that is in you."* By preparing ahead of time you will be ready to share your story, not only at your baptism but with anyone who may ask.

Your Personal Testimony

Take a few moments to write your personal testimony.
It will help you to formulate the story you will share
with anyone who asks about your faith in Jesus Christ.
Your testimony should be short and to-the-point. Here
are some guidelines:

Write one to three sentences about what your life was
like before you became a Christian. The purpose is not
to glorify your past, but give information that will help
people to relate to the person that you were.

_____

_____

_____

_____

_____

_____

_____

_____

Write one to three sentences describing how you came to the decision to give your life to Christ. What did that moment mean to you? Give the details of how or what you prayed so that the person you are speaking to will know how to invite Jesus into their own life.

_____

_____

_____

_____

_____

_____

_____

_____

_____

_____

_____

Write two or three paragraphs telling about the changes that you or others have seen in your life. Contrast these with what you were like before you became a Christian. You could also tell a story about how God has blessed you, healed you, or provided for you.

_____

_____

_____

_____

_____

_____

_____

_____

_____

_____

Common Questions About Baptism

Is water baptism the same as baptism in the Holy Spirit?

Baptism in water and baptism in the Holy Spirit are sometimes mentioned together in scripture and church tradition. Though often closely associated with one another, they are two different experiences (Acts 8:15-16). Baptism liturgies often blend the two into one experience. One is a physical act for the cleansing of sins and the removal of the fleshly sin nature; the other is a spiritual act which empowers the believer for Christian service. (Mark 1:8, John 1:33)

Baptism in the Holy Spirit is sometimes referred to as "the second blessing" because it typically follows baptism in water. Some churches believe that they should happen at the same time, and sometimes they do. However, we also see instances of people in the Bible who are baptized in the Holy Spirit either shortly before (Acts 10:44-48) or a longer time after water baptism (Acts 8:14-17, 19:2-6).

If you desire to be baptized in the Holy Spirit, simply ask God to give you this gift that Jesus talked about (John 14:16). Your Pastor or another Spirit-filled believer would gladly pray for you to receive this. The role of the Holy Spirit in the life of a believer should not be viewed as a one-time event; the scripture exhorts us to be continually filled with the Holy Spirit (Eph. 5:18).

Does baptism make me a member of the church?

Some churches equate baptism and church membership. Other churches do not. Those churches who baptize people into membership do so according to the tradition which was established by the early church, which was much easier to understand when there was only one expression of the church. Here are some reasons for keeping baptism and church membership separate:

1. A believer's first allegiance should be to Jesus; allegiance to the local church is secondary. The local church is part of the Body of Christ, not the whole Body. (The early church did not have this dilemma. Denominational divisions within the church happened around the end of the first millennium and escalated after the reformation.)

2. Baptized believers ought to identify themselves with all believers, all over the world, regardless of denomination, who call Jesus Christ their Lord and Savior.

3. A person should take the time to seriously consider church membership as a separate step of commitment. They should find out about the church and what is expected from a member. However, this should not delay their affirming their commitment to Christ.

Some churches may presume that by being baptized you intend to join the church. If you are not sure, you should ask. Whatever the case, you should know your church's membership requirements. If you are interested in becoming a member of your church, please request membership information from your church staff.

What will happen at your baptism?

We have talked about what baptism means and what your baptism means to you. It is normal to experience some nervousness about being baptized. This might simply be a fear of water, of being in front of people, or perhaps of not knowing what will happen. Perhaps you have never actually seen a baptism. I hope that by describing the event you will be mentally prepared and better able to appreciate the experience.

You should also be aware that Satan knows that

you are taking an important step in your Christian walk. You may experience some spiritual resistance in the form of distracting circumstances or unsettled thoughts or feelings. Your determination to press forward and receive baptism will send a message to our spiritual enemy that you are firm in your decision and that his tactics are useless. If you still have any questions about whether or not you want to be baptized, your pastor will be glad to talk with you about that.

In some cultural contexts where witchcraft or occult superstitions are prevalent, baptism becomes a time for declaring one's complete allegiance to Jesus Christ. In Thailand, for example, they would dispose of items or jewelry with occult meanings or symbols prior to being baptized. This context calls attention to the fact that baptism signifies a transfer of ownership from the kingdom of darkness to the Kingdom of God. For this reason also, some use this opportunity to pray a prayer of deliverance over the one being baptized

Someone might wonder what they can expect to experience when they are baptized. Will heaven open up and will a thunderous voice speak as when Jesus was baptized? (Matt. 3:16-17) Probably not, but you can expect to sense God's pleasure and affirmation. Some people experience dramatic healings and deliverance and other people do not. Most people experience the love and affirmation of the faith community, however, and consider it a time of joyous celebration. What happens to you should not be as important to you as your act of obedience to God.

The Baptism Service

Worship - The baptism service may or may not be part of a regular worship service. In any case it will likely include singing, prayer and preaching from the Bible, as do most services.

Preparation - At some point you will be instructed to prepare for baptism. If you are not already wearing the clothes in which you intend to be baptized, this is your cue to exit the sanctuary and change clothes. Be sure to remove watches, wallets and phones from your person. Some things should not be immersed in water!

Testimony - The pastor will call for the baptism candidates to come forward. One at a time, you will be asked to share your reason for wanting to be baptized, the story of your conversion, or some evidence of what God has done in your life. You may use portions of what you have written in this workbook as your testimony. If you are unable to speak because of nervousness, or overcome with emotion, someone else may be able to read what you have written on your behalf. If you would like to share something different from what you have written, please let your pastor know before the service.

Prayer - After everyone has given their testimony, candidates will, one by one, be invited into the water for baptism. A pastor or leader will be there to assist you. Before the actual baptism there will be a time for prayer and blessing. The pastor will pray for you, as may others in the congregation. Prophetic words often come forth at this time. If you have a spiritual mentor, it would be appropriate to mention it, so that they might be given the opportunity to pray also.

Baptism - When you enter the water it will come to about waist level on most people. The pastor will instruct you how to stand. Typically, you will stand with your arms crossed over your chest. You may hold your nose if you need to. The pastor (or elder or deacon) will place one arm behind you and the other on your crossed arms. He will say something like "Upon your confession of faith, I baptize you in the name of the Father, Son, and Holy Spirit in and through the power of Jesus Christ." At this time allow yourself to go down and backward, bending your knees slightly if you are a taller person. The pastor will assist you in going down and coming back up.

Celebration - As you come up out of the water you will be greeted by someone holding a robe or perhaps a towel that you brought. There will be singing and rejoicing. Family and friends will want to greet you. You may change into dry clothes or stay and witness others being baptized.

Practical Suggestions for the Baptismal Candidate

As you prepare for baptism here are some things you should know:

> Wear normal street clothes to be baptized in. Swimsuits or shorts may be appropriate for outdoor baptisms but are often not considered appropriate in the sanctuary.

> Select modest clothing that can get wet. Keep in mind that whites and even light colors are often transparent when wet and some fabrics might cling to your body.

> Jeans and heavy fabrics are usually the most modest. They are also more difficult to dry, but you will be allowed to change immediately afterward.

> Bring a large fluffy towel or a terrycloth bathrobe.

May God bless you as you prepare yourself for this special occasion!

End notes

1. Kostenberger, 2006, pp. 11-12

2. Bartholomew & Goheen, 2004, p. 133

3. "John's baptism was an insult to the Jewish establishment because it was not a rite of initiation. It assumed that active members of the Jewish community needed to be cleansed like proselytes, confessing their sins in anticipation of the judgment to come." (West, 1991, p. 18)

4. Jones has produced a contemporary translation of the Didache from which I am also quoting. (Jones, 2009, p. 5)

5. Didache' 7:1-4 (Jones, 2009, pp. 25-26)

6. Brown, 1965, p. 6

7. "The debates in the early church were not over adult baptism versus infant baptism, but believer's baptism versus paedobaptism." (McKinion, 2006, p. 164)

8. McKinion, pp. 171-173

9. Brown, 1965, pp. 26-27

10. This view states that the reality of the church is that it is covenantal and baptism is a participation in the mystery (sacrament) of this reality. (West, 1991, p. 31)

11. Aland, 1963, p. 106

12. Irvin & Sunquist, 2011, p. 335

13. According to Miller, Anabaptists reject the idea of sacrament as *ex opere operato* means of grace. (Miller, 1991, p. 45) This Latin phrase, which initially was understood to mean that sacraments were effective, even if administered by fallen leaders led to the belief that the church and its sacraments are the means by which God dispenses His grace. "Any under-standing of baptism which can be enacted not only independently of the believing response of faith and commitment, but even without emphasizing that believing response and commitment is an essential part of the divinely initiated covenantal transaction of which baptism is a sign, represents both a different understanding of divine grace and of sacramen-tal reality. (Miller, 1991, p. 48)

14. Horsch gives examples of statements by Luther, Melanchthon and Zwingli all stating that baptism is not effectual in saving a person and yet they continue to baptize infants fearing for their eternal status. (Horsch, 1917, pp. 13-18)

15. Irvin & Sunquist, 2012, p. 91

16. Yoder, 1527, 1973, p. 10

17. Irvin & Sunquist, 2012, p. 150

18. Augustine defined sacrament as "a visible form of an invisible grace." (Roth, 1960, p. 195)

19. Pilgram Marpeck, one of the early Anabaptist lead-ers- "God continues to be revealed in ways that are simultaneously spiritual and material." (Roth, 1960, pp. 202-203)

20. Mennonite Confession of Faith, 1963, p. 19

Pastor Joel Elton Kolb serves as Associate Pastor of Hopewell Christian Fellowship in Telford, PA. His responsibilities include preaching, pastoral counseling and oversight of various ministries such as Men's Ministry and Life Groups. He has been married to his wife Heidi for more than 27 years. They have four children and reside in Sellersville, PA. Heidi is also gifted in leadership and administration and works at the church.

Joel is passionate about world missions, leadership development, and helping people find healing. He and Heidi began their ministry as missionaries to Denmark, where they also lived for more than 3 years. He has travelled over the entire northern hemisphere from England to Russia. Currently, he and his wife are involved with providing pastoral care to missionaries in Thailand and Belize, as well as serving as a liaison for the Hopewell Network to Haiti and India. He also serves the Hopewell Network by assisting at the Dove/ Hopewell Leadership Training School.

Joel and Heidi are 1990 graduates of Christ For the Nations Institute, Stony Brook. In 2014 he also completed an MDiv. from Biblical Seminary in Hatfield, Pa. He has earned certifications in Christian

Counseling from Biblical Seminary and from Global Trauma Recovery Institute. Much of his time is devoted to pastoral counseling and inner healing ministry in the church, in the community, and around the world.

You can visit Pastor Joel and Heidi at:

www.CleanHeartInternational.org

Baptisms in India – held indoors without singing or celebration because of intense persecution.
~Photo courtesy of Kedar Kapoor.

Baptism in Thailand where believers are eager to identify with Jesus even though they will face social opposition. At this baptism some of the observers who were previously seekers asked to be baptized, also declaring that they are following Jesus.

~Photographs courtesy of Dwane Reitz.

For Bulk Ordering Information
please contact us at:

Info@EndlessPress.org

EndlessPress.org

Manufactured by Amazon.ca
Bolton, ON